PAUL CARDALL
RETURN HOME

01	IMMIGRANT SHIPS
03	SHROPSHIRE HILLS
07	LOVE ONE ANOTHER
10	AN EVENING IN PARIS
14	RED POPPY FIELDS
18	CASTLES AND CATHEDRALS
23	ELIZA'S THEME
27	SHORES OF NORMANDY
29	LAND OF OUR ANCESTORS
32	I BELIEVE IN CHRIST
35	LJUBLJANA	HEART OF SLOVENIA
38	RETURN HOME
40	FATHERS AND DAUGHTERS

Immigrant Ships

Paul Cardall

Shropshire Hills

Paul Cardall

Love One Another

Luacine Clark Fox

www.paulcardall.com
©2023 All Heart Publishing, LLC

An Evening in Paris

Paul Cardall

www.paulcardall.com
©2023 All Heart Publishing, LLC

An Evening in Paris

An Evening in Paris

Red Poppy Fields

Paul Cardall

www.paulcardall.com
©2023 All Heart Publishing, LLC

Red Poppy Fields 15

Red Poppy Fields

Castles and Cathedrals

Paul Cardall

www.paulcardall.com
©2023 All Heart Publishing, LLC

Castles and Cathedrals

Castles and Cathedrals 21

Eliza's Theme

Eliza's Theme

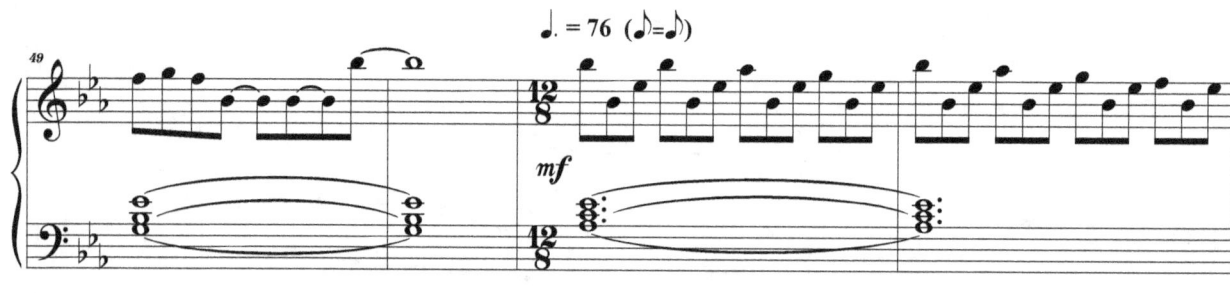

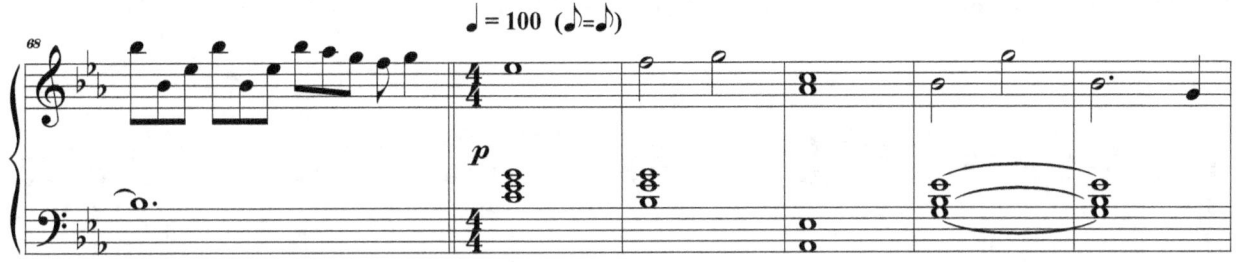

Shores of Normandy

Paul Cardall

Land of Our Ancestors

Paul Cardall

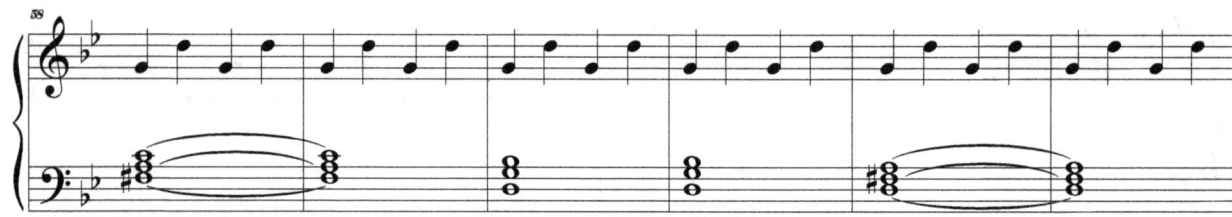

I Believe In Christ

Gleefully ♩ = 88

John Longhurst

Ljubljana
Heart of Slovenia

Paul Cardall

www.paulcardall.com
©2023 All Heart Publishing, LLC

Return Home

Paul Cardall

Return Home

39

TRANSCRIBED BY ALEX BROWN

FOR ADDITIONAL MUSIC AND INFORMATION SUBSCRIBE TO

WWW.PAULCARDALL.COM

COPYRIGHT 2023 ALL HEART PUBLISHING, LLC

MAKING COPIES IS ILLEGAL

www.ingramcontent.com/pod-product-compliance
Lightning Source LLC
Chambersburg PA
CBHW081409070526
44583CB00020B/2744